CHEERLEADING

COMPETITIVE CHEERLEADING

By Carla Mooney

SportsZone
An Imprint of Abdo Publishing
abdobooks.com

abdobooks.com

Published by Abdo Publishing, a division of ABDO, PO Box 398166, Minneapolis, Minnesota 55439.

Printed in the United States of America, North Mankato, Minnesota
052024
092024

THIS BOOK CONTAINS RECYCLED MATERIALS

Cover Photo: Scott Winters/Icon Sportswire/AP Images
Interior Photos: Romané Salazar/Flickr, 4–5; Joseph Calomeni/iStockphoto, 7; Phelan M. Ebenhack/AP Images, 8–9, 12, 22–23, 29; Cherednychenko Ihor/Shutterstock Images, 10, 21, 25; Jacek Makowicz/Alamy, 15; H. Mark Weidman Photography/Alamy, 16–17; John Fisher/Cal Sport Media/AP Images, 19; Jens Wolf/picture-alliance/dpa/AP Images, 26; Dov Makabaw/Alamy, 28

Editor: Christa Kelly
Series Designer: Kate Liestman

Library of Congress Control Number: 2023949402

Library of Congress Cataloging-in-Publication Data

Names: Mooney, Carla, author.
Title: Competitive cheerleading / by Carla Mooney
Description: Minneapolis, Minnesota: Abdo Publishing, 2025 | Series: Cheerleading | Includes online resources and index.
Identifiers: ISBN 9781098293529 (lib. bdg.) | ISBN 9798384912798 (ebook)
Subjects: LCSH: Cheerleading--Juvenile literature. | Competition (Psychology) in sports--Juvenile literature. | Sports--Juvenile literature.
Classification: DDC 791.6--dc23

TABLE OF CONTENTS

CHAPTER 1

COMPETING IN CHEERLEADING

Spotlights swirl in the gym. A squad of cheerleaders runs onto the mat. Each one wears a matching sparkling uniform. The cheerleaders move into their starting positions.

Boom! The music blasts, and the squad bursts into movement. The cheerleaders flip and twist through a series of tumbling passes. They perform cartwheels and stunts in unison. Every step is part of a choreographed routine.

At some competitions, cheerleaders perform for more than 50,000 spectators!

ARDINALS

The team strikes a pose as the music stops. The crowd roars in applause. The cheerleaders run from the mat, both excited and nervous. Did they win the competition? They will have to wait to find out.

CHEERLEADING

Cheerleading is an exciting activity. Cheerleaders perform difficult tumbling skills, jumps, and stunts. They spend hours practicing routines with challenging choreography.

There are different types of cheerleaders. Some cheerleaders are part of a school team. They perform cheers and stunts at their school's athletic events. These performances help energize crowds and athletes. Some school cheerleading teams also compete against teams from other schools.

Other cheerleaders are part of All Star cheer teams. All Star is a division of cheerleading that is led by an organization called the U.S. All Star Federation. All Star teams focus on perfecting their routines for competitions.

During competitions, cheerleading squads perform complicated routines for judges. These routines are normally only a few minutes long, but cheerleaders pack a lot of skills into that short time.

The judges are trained to evaluate the routines. They award points for aspects such as synchronized moves and good technique while deducting points for mistakes such as safety violations and missteps. At the end of the competition, the team with the most points wins.

Preparing for a competition takes months of training, but the result is worth the effort. Competitions are a way to showcase a team's hard work and skill. They're among the most exciting parts of being a cheerleader.

It can be expensive to participate in competitive cheerleading.

CHAPTER 2

HISTORY OF COMPETITIVE CHEER

Cheerleading was invented more than 100 years ago. The first known organized cheer was performed in 1884 at Princeton University when a group of football fans shouted a rehearsed cheer from the stands.

In 1898, cheering moved from the stands to the field. At a University of Minnesota football game, a student named Johnny Campbell jumped from his

All Star cheerleaders typically attend five to 10 competitions each year.

SCOTS

seat and ran down to the football field. He led the student body in a cheer for Minnesota's team.

Soon, many college sporting events had people on the sidelines to lead the crowd in cheers. These students were known as yell leaders. As cheering evolved, yell leaders began using megaphones to

Today, cheerleading is popular around the world.

make their cheers louder. They started signaling the crowd with rehearsed arm motions. Some carried signs and pom-poms. Others performed simple jumps and gymnastics skills.

By the 1920s, most high schools and colleges in the United States had cheerleaders. At first, most cheerleaders were men. This changed during World War II (1939–1945). Many young men were drafted to fight in the war. Women took their place leading crowds in cheers. By the late 1940s, most cheerleaders were women. Today, about 85 percent of these athletes are women.

CHEER COMPETITIONS

The International Cheerleading Foundation held the first cheerleading competitions in the 1960s. College teams performed routines for judges, competing to win awards. The routines included simple stunts and tumbling skills. Each year, the best teams earned a spot on the foundation's prestigious Top Ten College Cheerleading Squads list.

In 1978, the Collegiate Cheerleading Championships aired on television. People nationwide watched the top college squads perform and saw that competitive cheerleading

The National Cheerleaders Association hosts the biggest cheerleading competition in the world.

was more than just sideline chants. Interest in cheerleading grew, and competitions became even more impressive. Cheerleaders became more athletic, each team working to outperform the competitors. They showed off their strength and flexibility with increasingly difficult stunts, jumps, and tumbling skills.

In 1982, the first National Cheerleading Championship was held and shown live on television. Soon after, the first All Star cheer programs began. At first, All Star teams competed at school cheer competitions. Later, competitions were created specifically for All Star teams.

Today, hundreds of cheer competitions are held each year. There are regional, national, and

SAFETY GUIDELINES

Several organizations create cheer rules and safety guidelines. The American Association of Cheerleading Coaches and Advisors published its first safety manual in 1990. It also created a training course for coaches. Today, USA Cheer and the U.S. All Star Federation work to create rules and safety guidelines for cheerleading and cheer competitions.

international competitions. Different competitions are held for a variety of skill levels and ages.

STUNT

In 2011, a new type of cheer competition called STUNT was created. In a traditional cheer competition, several teams compete, with each team performing a two-and-a-half-minute routine. In STUNT competitions, two cheer teams compete against each other. STUNT competitions are divided into four events called quarters. Each quarter tests a different skill. The quarters include partner stunts, pyramids and tosses, group jumps and tumbling, and team performance.

During the first three quarters, the two competing teams simultaneously perform an identical, preassigned routine. The team that best performs the routine wins the round. During the final event, each team takes turns performing a routine that combines the skills performed in the previous quarters. Since its invention, STUNT has exploded in popularity. Today, it is one of the fastest-growing female sports in the United States.

Though STUNT is considered a sport by athletic associations, regular cheerleading is not.

CHAPTER 3

PREPARING FOR COMPETITION

Cheerleading takes a lot of strength, stamina, and flexibility. During practices, cheerleaders strengthen their bodies and learn new skills, all under the careful supervision of coaches. Most teams practice four or five times each week, with each practice lasting up to three hours. It can take months of training for cheerleaders to prepare for a competition.

Advanced cheerleaders know dozens of skills.

KNIGHTS
KNIGHTS
KNIGHTS

FITNESS TRAINING

Exercising is one of the most important parts of practice. Different exercises strengthen cheerleaders in different ways. Cardio exercises such as running and biking build endurance. Strength training exercises such as weight lifting help cheerleaders perform stunts and tumbling skills. Stretches help cheerleaders prevent injuries and gain flexibility.

During practices, coaches also teach cheerleaders new skills. These skills include stunts,

STUNTS

Each cheerleader in a stunt has a role. The cheerleaders at the bottom of a stunt are called the bases. They support the cheerleader at the top of the stunt, also known as the flyer. In some stunts, another cheerleader is in charge of helping the flyer stay safe and balanced. This person is called the back spot.

Complex tumbling skills should be learned under the supervision of a qualified adult.

dance moves, tumbling skills, and jumps. When put together, these skills form elaborate routines.

ROUTINES

Once cheerleaders have mastered individual skills, they can begin practicing their routines. A winning routine is challenging and exciting. It grabs the judges' attention. It showcases the team's athletic and cheerleading skills.

Routines combine stunts, jumps, tumbling skills, and dance moves. Each part of the routine must flow seamlessly into the next section. Competition routines are created with each event's specific scoring criteria in mind.

Coaches usually choreograph a team's routines. Some teams hire a professional choreographer. Experienced team members can also help with choreography. Choreographers often pair routines with music. This helps the cheerleaders stay synchronized. Choreographers may also add props such as signs, poms, and megaphones to cheerleaders' routines.

Props must be approved by competition staff before being used.

CHAPTER 4

COMPETITION DAY

There are competitions for cheerleaders of all ages and skills. Some competitions are for school cheer teams. Other competitions are for All Star cheer teams. Squads usually compete against other teams of the same age and skill.

At the start of each cheer season, coaches pick the best competitions for their teams. Competitions vary in size

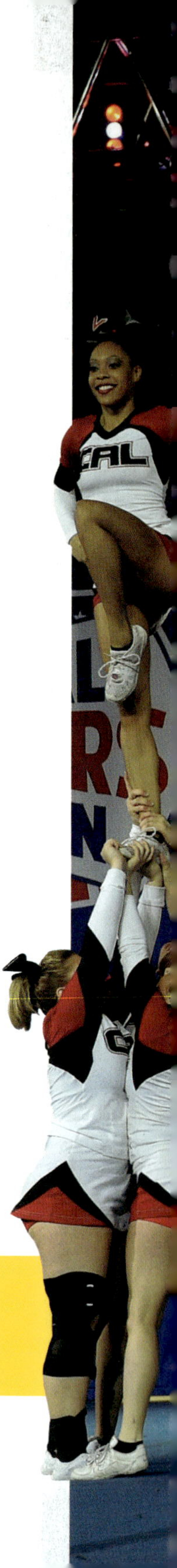

Cheer competitions are usually held from late fall to early spring.

CAL
CAL
CAL
NCA

and location. Some are small, one-day events. Others are larger, multiday competitions.

GETTING READY

Competitions can take place anywhere from small high school gyms to large stadiums or theater stages. When cheerleaders arrive, they warm up and stretch. Then they practice stunts and tumbling passes. While they wait for their turn to compete, they may watch other teams perform.

As their performance time gets closer, the cheerleaders get dressed in their uniforms.

ALL STAR LEVELS

All Star competitions are divided into seven levels. Each level allows teams to perform specific skills. The highest level is level seven. Teams competing in level seven are allowed to perform the most challenging skills.

Cheerleaders should smile and act confident throughout their routines.

Then they run through their entire routine. Finally, the team heads to the back of the stage and the cheerleaders wait for their turn to perform.

SCORING POINTS

Once their team is called, the cheerleaders run onto the competition floor and get into their opening

Different competitions have different rules regarding what skills cheerleaders are allowed to perform.

positions. The music blasts, and the team springs into action. The cheerleaders perform their routine, taking care to remain synchronized with the music.

A panel of judges watches the team's every move. Many judges are former cheerleaders or coaches. They evaluate the team's performance. In some competitions, each judge rates a team's routine separately. During other competitions, each judge is assigned to watch a different aspect of the routine, such as jumps or tumbling.

Judges use score sheets to award points. The criteria on score sheets can vary by competition. Most score sheets have sections where judges can award points for stunts, jumps, tumbling, and overall performance. Cheerleaders can earn higher scores by attempting more difficult skills. Judges also award points for creativity and showmanship.

If a team makes a mistake, the judges deduct points. Mistakes include poor landings, falls, and failure to stay synchronized. Deductions are also given for breaking safety rules.

After every team has performed, the judges total the score sheets. The team with the most points is the winner. The judges announce the winning teams for each skill level.

Judges evaluate a team's technique as the cheerleaders perform skills.

Competitive cheerleading has become a popular activity worldwide. Tori Rubin is the co-owner of Unity Allstar, a competitive cheer gym in London, United Kingdom. She explained why she loves cheerleading. "It's a great sport because it's teamwork," she said. "It's all about athletes working together in unison to create something spectacular."

Though cheerleading is hard work, perfecting a routine makes the effort worth it.

GLOSSARY

cardio
Exercises that increase a person's heart and breathing rates to make their heart and lungs stronger.

choreographed
Something that has been planned, often referring to a routine.

choreographer
Someone who creates routines for dancers or cheerleaders.

endurance
A person's ability to keep doing something.

evaluate
To determine how good something is.

megaphone
A cone-shaped prop used to make someone's voice louder.

pom-pom
A ball-shaped prop usually made of shiny pieces of plastic or foil.

pyramid
A cheerleading skill in which two or more stunts are connected by the flyers.

routine
A performance made up of individual stunts, tumbling moves, jumps, and dance moves.

squad
A cheerleading team.

stamina
The ability to perform physical exercise for an extended time.

stunt
A skill in which a cheerleader is supported above the ground by one or more teammates.

synchronized
Performed at the same time as another person.

technique
The way a skill is performed.

tumbling
Gymnastics skills such as cartwheels and flips.

unison
Performed by a group at the same time.

MORE INFORMATION

BOOKS

Banks, Anita. *Cheer Tryouts and Training*. Abdo, 2025.

James, India. *Cheer Skills and Drills*. Abdo, 2025.

Troupe, Thomas Kingsley. *Cheerleading*. Crabtree, 2022.

ONLINE RESOURCES

Booklinks
NONFICTION NETWORK
FREE! ONLINE NONFICTION RESOURCES

To learn more about competitive cheerleading, please visit abdobooklinks.com or scan this QR code. These links are routinely monitored and updated to provide the most current information available.

INDEX

ABOUT THE AUTHOR

Carla Mooney is a graduate of the University of Pennsylvania with a degree in economics. Today, she writes for young people and is the author of many books for young adults and children.